Connect With Jesus

A Discipleship Workbook by Don Babin

A Discipleship Workbook
By Don Babin

After serving in the ministry of evangelism for over 35 years I felt like there was a need for some basic principles of Christianity. Together with my wife Michelle we have seen right at about 100,000 professions of faith from corner to corner of the United States and other countries of the world. Many of these new believers had nothing put in their hands to help them get started in their new relationship with Jesus.

Michelle and I served God 16 years of evangelism, 14 years as founder and pastor of a Church and now 5 years as a missionary evangelist among the Maasai tribe of East Africa. While we were pastoring we saw a huge need for a workbook that was easy and basic. This workbook is the results of many years of reaching people for Jesus.

This is by no means to replace having a home church with personal relationships with other believers. It is simply a good start for any believer. As a matter of fact it would not hurt for a mature believer to review the basics in this book. No one departs from the fundamentals. All NBA players practice the fundaments, in the world we never get away from reading, writing and arithmetic, these are the fundamentals of life. In Christianity we should always be reviewing the basics to keep us rooted and grounded.

It is Michelle and my prayer this book is used freely by everyone who needs a good start in their beliefs. We have even had it translated into the Maassai language and use it way in the bush of Africa. Check it out and send me a personal email if it has been useful in your life.

God bless you and be radical for Jesus.

This manual is dedicated to my two boys, Dustin and Carman, who have proven there is more, and who love Jesus and have dedicated their lives to living and loving Jesus. You have made your dad so proud. You are the joy of my life.

I also dedicate this book to Michelle, my wife, who is also the love of my life. Michelle, you have been the most wonderful gift next to my salvation. I cannot imagine life without you. Thanks for just being you. These three people are a constant reminder we will spend forever together in heaven.

These three people are daily proof to me that the power of God is real every day to keep that which we have committed unto Him against that day. God is really good all the time. Walk with Him daily, don't just take a walk with Him, but walk with Him.

To those who have made this book possible:
My wife, who has been such a support and always willing for me to take the time to do what God has put on my heart. – Like take the time to put this workbook together.

To John Hovda, who has been very paitient and has taken great time to make this workbook look as good as it does. Thanks John, for helping us put something into new believer's hands. You are a blessing to our ministry.

Congratulations

You have just made the most important decisions of your whole life and eternity. By giving charge of your life over to Jesus Christ, and allowing Him to be your Savior, and take over control of your life you will now begin to experience a brand new life.

Therefore, if any man be in Christ, He is a new creation, old things will pass away, and behold all things have become new.
2 Corinthians 5:17

You are now beginning an exciting journey of spiritual growth as a child of God begin your spiritual stronger you are in the Lord, the more fun be. It will not always be a life without difficulty, but He will be in every difficulty with you. Wow, isn't that awesome. He can calm the storm if He chooses or use the storm to strengthen your relationship with Him. So how do you grow in you new relationship with the God of the universe?

Connect With Jesus is designed to help answer that question. You need a Bible and a pen to fill in the blanks as you study your Bible. Make sure to look up the Bible references. You might even want to highlight them in your Bible. This is a way to get more of the Word of God hidden in your heart.

> Thy word have I laid up in mine heart, that I might not sin against thee.
> Psalms 119:11

Take the time to fill in each blank in your book.

Your Bible is divided into sections. The first section is called the **Old Testament**, containing 39 separate books. The second section is the **New Testament**, containing 27 books. Most books are divided into chapters and verses. There are several good modern translations of the Bible that are helpful to understanding the Bible. Ask your pastor which translation would be a good one for you to read and use for this study book.

This is just the beginning of your exciting journey with an awesome God who is crazy in love with you. He is so excited about you getting to know Him better. Make it a part of your life to enjoy your journey with your loving God and Savior.

Take time to pray as your study this book and your Bible. You have come into a brand new life in Jesus. You now belong to Jesus. But there is more! Can you believe it? There is more! Your new discoveries will surprise you on a regular basis. Get ready!

Foreword

"WHOEVER LOVES DISCIPLINE, LOVES KNOWLEDGE."

Discipline is the key to success. Living a disciplined life requires much more than a dream or a desire, it demands sacrifice and determination. The word "discipline" comes from the word "disciple." I believe if you want to be a faithful follower of Jesus, then you must apply some discipline. If you want knowledge about how to walk with Jesus, you must love discipline to gain that knowledge.

As you grow in Jesus and obey Him, you will begin to discover your new found freedom 

from anxiety, jealousy, fear, irritation, boredom, hatred, unforgivingness, bitterness and all the things that will try to hold you back from the abundant life. I have served the Lord for quite a few years and I know that what you are about to learn will not only change your life for the present, but will also give you what you need to face EVERY difficulty in life. This short manual will point you in the direction of becoming the champion Jesus sees in you.

The necessities for developing a dynamic Christian life are covered in this Connect With Jesus discipleship material. I know from over thirty years of experience, if you strive to be faithful to these basics, you will achieve a life full and rich with the blessings of God. As with anything worth something, you must be determined to discipline your life and set aside time to develop your inner man. I am sure that right now you have the desire to be all you can be in Jesus. As a matter of fact, you are probably ready to "charge hell with a water pistol" That's great! I wish every believer was as fired up as you are right now.

> *The time is coming when God will test your faith, to enable it to grow James 1:2-4*

You should look those verses up and read them. It will bless your socks off, even with your shoes on. The basics you are about to learn will help you prepare for trials and tribulations you will have.

> *These things have I spoken unto you, that in me ye may have peace. In the world ye shall have tribulation: but be good cheer, I have overcome the world. John 16:33*

Make a commitment to finish this material, all the way to the end.

Lesson 1

KNOWING THAT YOU KNOW

It is vitally important that you "**know that you know**" you have come into a personal relationship with Jesus. You need to be able to say without hesitation, "if I died right now, there is no doubt in my heart and mind that I would go to Heaven!" Until you have completely settled this in your heart and mind, you will always struggle and your spiritual growth will be hindered greatly. The Bible says:

> *Therefore if any man be in Christ, he becomes a new creation, old things pass away and behold all things become new.*
> *2 Corinthians 5:17*

The Bible clearly says when you get saved you will become a "**new creation**." This word "creation," means a new "species." A new species is like changing from a dog to an elephant. Now that is what I call change. If you went from a poodle to a great Dane, that is pretty big change. But to change from a dog to an elephant, is way beyond anyone's imagination. That is the kind of change the Bible says will happen to us when we get saved. God's word

11

clearly states that salvation brings huge change to our life. So if God changes us in such a drastic way when we get saved, how can we go through such a drastic change and not know it. You see, if God changes you from a dog to an elephant, I believe you would know it immediately. You would look at yourself with surprise and say, "**WOW, look what happened to me**."

When a person comes into the saving knowledge of Jesus Christ, he will totally rearrange his/her life. Priorities will change, ambitions will change, and many other areas of his/her life will be totally transformed. When the God of this universe comes to live inside of you, to make His home in you, and go everywhere you go, you cannot help but know He is there. God in all of His glory, power, majesty and personhood moves to make his home in your life. WOW, that is spectacular! How can the God of Glory, come and make His home inside of you and you not know it. The whole letter of First John was written so a believer can know without doubt, that he knows he/she is saved.

> *I write these things to you who believe in the name of the Son of God so that you may know that you have eternal life. 1 John 5:13*

GET TO FIRST BASE

I heard a story about a baseball player who got a great hit and ran all the bases. As he slid into home plate, the catcher tagged him with his glove. Just as he tagged the runner, he dropped the ball out of his catchers mitt. The catcher quickly scooped up the ball, hoping the umpire did not see him drop it. The umpire yelled, "You're out!" The crowd had witnessed the catcher dropping the ball and began to yell, "No, the catcher dropped the ball!" There was such a commotion the ump had to stop the game and go to a microphone and inform the crowd that he saw the catcher drop the ball, but that the man was not out at home but out at first, because he failed to tag first base. This is true of so many church members. They go to church, get baptized, attend Sunday school and go through all the right motions. One day they will go sliding into home and God will say, "You are out!" What a shock to think all your life you will go home to be with Jesus and yet God will call you out, because you failed to tag first base, which is really being born again. This first lesson in your manual is to make sure that according to scripture, you have truly tagged first base. You need to be able to say, "I know that I know, if I died today I would go home and be with Jesus forever." Once you settle this eternal issue, you will be ready to begin an awesome adventure of spiritual growth. Let's begin your first lesson in your Connect With Jesus discipleship book.

KNOWING THAT I KNOW

You may be like me. When I was saved, I did not know any Bible teachings on salvation, or any other evangelical subject for that matter. That's okay. Although these truths must be a part of your salvation experience, it is NOT the knowledge of the things that save you. It was not until later in my walk with Jesus that I was able to reflect upon these Biblical truths and find each in my salvation experience. It is kind of like eating a really delicious pie. You may not know the ingredients, but you can still enjoy the pie. These are five extremely important ingredients that must be a part of anyone's salvation experience in order for it to be real. And by the way, all of these ingredients can take place in just a second or it can be a process taking days or even months.

Answer this question: If I were to die right now, do I know for sure I would go to Heaven?

How do I know this?

Read 1 John 5:13.
John wrote this letter so that the reader might know what?

According to this verse, is it possible to know for sure that you are saved and have a relationship with Jesus?

Read 2 Corinthians 5:17.
According to this verse, what happens to a person when they get saved?

INGREDIENT #1

The Holy Spirit must initiate your salvation experience.

In John 15:16, who chose you?

In Matthew 16:17, who revealed the truth to Peter?

In Philippians 1:6, who begins the good work in us?

This is just a few verses out of many in the Bible that shows God initiating the salvation of people. God not only does the saving, but He is also the one who calls us to Himself. It is by the Holy Spirit that He reveals the truth to us and shows us we need to be saved. Our part is to respond to the work He does. You have a free will to cooperate with what God wants to do in your life or to reject Him. The choice is yours. Getting saved is not about making mom or dad happy. Salvation is not about following the crowd or reverse peer pressure. A person cannot be talked into being saved or scared into being saved unless the Holy Spirit is drawing that person. What I am trying to say is this, "God must begin the good work." God must draw you to Himself. Many times as the Holy Spirit is calling us to salvation, we lose interest in the things we once thought were very important. The Holy Spirit will convict us or convince us that our lifestyle is not pleasing to Jesus. The Holy Spirit will show us that something vital is missing in our lives. You may experience a sense of emptiness. You might even come to the place where what once pleased you no longer has the luster it had. You may become very displeased with where your life is heading. Most of the time this is how the Holy Spirit prepares us to open our hearts to His work in us.

Read John 16:8. This verse points out three things the Holy Spirit does in our lives. List these three things in the space provided below:

When the Holy Spirit begins His work in your life, He will point out that you have sinned. To sin means to "miss the mark." This means you have missed the mark God has had for your life. When the Spirit shows you this sinfulness in your life, you will sense a deep need for the Savior Jesus Christ. Jesus Christ because He is crazy in love with you, died on the cross so you would not have to be judged for your sinfulness. Isn't it awesome that God loves us enough to show us our need for Him. Stop right now and just thank God for showing you your need for Jesus Christ. This brings us to the second ingredient.

INGREDIENT # 2:

You must see your sin as a serious matter. Read Romans 6:23. How does this verse point out the seriousness of sin?

Read Romans 3:23. How does this verse tell you that you have a sin problem?

When Jesus died on the cross, He took **ALL** of your sin upon Himself so you would not have to suffer the consequences. He paid the price and suffered the penalty of your sin in your place. He became your sin and took it to the cross. Read 2 Corinthians 5:21. Jesus took **EVERY** sin you ever committed upon His flesh on the cross. The Bible calls this being "**justified**." A neat way of understanding what it means to be justified is to think of it as, "just as if I never sinned". Jesus took your sin upon Himself so He could take it to the cross in His flesh and pay the price instead of you paying. The Good News is Jesus died in your place to wipe your sin record completely clean. **WOW,** just think, you are as innocent as a new born baby. You are totally forgiven. Jesus loves you enough to take your place. Sin must be punished according to the justice of a Holy God. So instead of you being judged for your sin, He took your judgment and suffered in your place. Now, that is real **LOVE!** Take some time right now to thank God for what He did for you and then thank Him for making you clean from all sin. Now we come to the third ingredient.

INGREDIENT #3:

God will give you a measure of faith.

Read Romans 12:3 & Hebrews 12:2. These verses clearly state that:

God is the [________] and [________] of our faith.

This means God is the one who gives us our faith. He is the One who gives us our first measure of faith. It is up to us to choose to use our faith and to grow our faith. We can use our faith, causing it to grow, or not use it, causing it to wither and remain sick and weak. One of the ways we can cause our faith to grows is to study His Word (Romans 10:17). This is why it is important to let the Word of God get inside of you. Your faith will also grow as you go through the trials of life (James 1 :2-3).

Hebrews 12:2 also says He is the [________] of our faith.

This means He not only begins our faith, but He also is the [________]

He also tests our faith, read James 1: 1-4. According to this passage we should [________] when God tests our [________]

Bible faith is about the heart not the head. There is a big difference in believing with your heart and believing with your head. That difference is not just 12 inches. Read Romans 10:9-10.

In this passage we are to believe with our [ ]
Read James 2:14. What kind of faith saves a person according to this passage of scripture?

Let's have a quick review.
In the passage below, list the first three ingredients that are critical to a person's salvation.

THE REAL DEAL:

When you believe with your heart, it brings you into a personal relationship with Jesus. When you believe with your head, you just know more about Him.

I don't know a lot about electricity. I just know if you hit the switch on the wall the light comes on. I do know this much in my head about electricity: Suppose I stood on a chair in a bucket of water and stuck my finger in the light socket.

Then when someone turned on the switch I would really **know** electricity. Because that time, I experienced electricity.

That is the difference between head faith and heart faith. One kind of faith just knows about Jesus. However, saving faith is not just knowing about Him, but this kind of faith brings us into an experience with Jesus. A saving, knowing, life-changing relationship with Him.

We must use the kind of faith that brings us into a life-changing relationship. I have a dear friend who was going to church 9 months before he was born. He was raised in church, been to camps, revivals and all the other church functions all his life. He was a youth pastor and at age 27 applied the right kind of faith and was born again. He believed all those years in Jesus, but he did not believe with his heart. He had head knowledge but not heart felt faith.

You can believe in all the facts about Jesus and not be saved. This friend of mine believed Jesus died his whole life, but at age 27 he believed Jesus died for him. There is a big difference. Being saved is not believing in all the right things, it is believing in such a way, that your faith brings you into a personal relationship with Jesus Christ as Lord. If the faith you have does not change your life than your faith is not saving faith.

Can you review your salvation experience and find these ingredients? You may not have been aware of the terms or wording I use, but you should be able to identify them in some way or another.

INGREDIENT #4:

You must confess and repent of your sin.
Confess means, "to acknowledge." In other words, you acknowledge the fact that you have sinned against God. It is important that you see how your sin has broken God's heart, and want to come clean and change the way you think. I don't think we need to spend a lot of time on this ingredient. It is pretty obvious that every one of us have broken God's laws and have been marked with sin. This ingredient in your Connect With Jesus includes confessing or acknowledging the fact that you have sinned.

Read Romans 3:23. What does this verse say about who has sinned?

Most people do not have a problem with the "acknowledging or confessing," of sin. It is easy for us to agree with God that we are sinners. But, when it comes to the "repenting," part of salvation, lots of people miss God.

It is impossible to be saved without repentance. To repent means to "change your mind in such a way that it changes the direction of your life."

When the Holy Spirit begins His work in you, the first thing He shows you is your sin. By the way the Holy Spirit is very persistent. Even though you may resist His work at first, you will soon begin to realize you have a major problem and must be rescued by Jesus and Him alone. Once you are convinced of your sin problem, faith will come into play that Jesus is your answer. Once you see your sin problem due to the Holy Spirit doing His work in you, at the same time faith rises up in you to believe. You will begin to see by spiritual revelation how much Jesus loves you.

When you, by faith come to the understanding that God loves you so much He sent Jesus to take care of your sin issue, you will have a desire to love Him in return by a total surrender of your life to follow Him.

What an honor. Just stop and think for a moment. God loves you so much he took the punishment of your sin upon Himself in the form of Jesus Christ. He died on a cruel cross for you, so you would not have to suffer the punishment of your own sin. You will believe this in such a way, that you become willing to turn away from one lifestyle and live for Jesus. Your thinking will change about sin, God, your purpose, and every area of life. This is what repentance is all about. This is God changing your mind through faith.

Now that you have agreed with God about your sin and you have repented, let's look at a few scriptures.

Read Matthew 3:2. What was John the Baptist's main message in this passage of scripture?

Read Matthew 4:17. What was Jesus preaching?

Read Mark 6:12. What were the disciples teaching?

Read Luke 24:47. What was to be preached to all people?

Read Acts 2:38. When Peter preached at Pentecost, what did he command all men to do?

Read Acts 17:30. What does God command all men to do?

Read 2 Peter 3:9. It is God's desire for all men to do what?

So what does all this mean to you? It means once God begins His work in you and has given you a measure of faith, the automatic response is for you to turn away from your past lifestyle, by your thinking being changed, and to begin to live for Jesus.

This does not mean you will be perfect in your living. It means you will hate sin and desire to please God with the way you live. When you come to Jesus, you should turn away from anything that is displeasing to God and give Him your whole heart and life. Don't hold anything back from Him. Repent of your sinful lifestyle and turn away from all sin and evil. Now for the last ingredient!

INGREDIENT #5:

You must surrender your life to the lordship of Jesus Christ.

Jesus is referred to as "**Lord**" at least **610** times in the New Testament, and only **37** times as '**Savior**'. Jesus is called 'Lord' throughout the book of Acts, but is only called "Savior" twice. What are Christians talking about when they refer to Jesus as Lord? What does this mean? First of all, let's look at the word "Lord." A lord is someone who rules a kingdom. In England, they still have lords who are leaders.

Nowhere in the Bible does it tell of men asking Jesus to be their Savior. Being saved means Jesus Christ becomes LORD of your life. Yes, Jesus is the Savior of the world. However, for Jesus to become your Savior, you must allow Him to take charge of your life and be your Lord, master, or boss.

Jesus is Lord of His Kingdom. He is the absolute ruler of the Kingdom of God. When someone says that Jesus is Lord of their life, they are saying they have been Born Again and now are under the leadership of Jesus Christ.

Salvation is changing from living your life for self to Jesus taking charge. Now real life begins. You will discover purpose and joy unspeakable. Knowing Jesus as the boss of your life will fulfill you like nothing else can in the whole world. Jesus fills your emptiness in a way that only He can do.

Read Acts 2:21. Peter preached that everyone who called upon who, would be saved?

Read Acts 16:31. In this verse of scripture, who do we need to believe in to be saved?

Read Romans 10:9-10. What does this verse tell us confess in order for someone to be saved?

Salvation is being able to say, or confess that Jesus Christ is Lord of your life.

CHECKLIST:

Now let's review one more time.

When you bake a cake and leave out just one ingredient you change the way the cake is supposed to turn out. It is vital these ingredients be a part of your salvation experience. Remember the words are not important. Below is a checklist to check out each ingredient and make sure they are a part of your experience with Jesus.

1. Do you remember when the Holy Spirit began to "tug on your heart" and call you to Jesus?

☐ yes   ☐ no

2. Do you remember when you realized you had a serious problem with sin and wanted to be forgiven and come clean with God?

☐ yes   ☐ no

3. Do you remember when God started giving you a measure of faith? You started believing Jesus died for YOUR sin and you began to follow and serve Jesus?

☐ yes   ☐ no

4. Do you remember when you made a decision to turn away from sin and ask Jesus to forgive you? You acknowledged your sin - you hated it so much, you wanted Jesus totally?

☐ *yes*   ☐ *no*

5. Have you surrendered your life to the control of Jesus and declared Him Lord of your life?

☐ *yes*   ☐ *no*

PRAISE GOD if you answered yes to all these questions. If you have a problem with any of these questions, you should talk with your pastor or send me an e-mail with your question donbabin@gmail.com. Please remember, we are dealing with your eternity, your forever!

You have just completed session one of your basic training. Once you settle your eternal issue, you can move on to your spiritual growth. The rest of this manual will help you to jump start your adventure with Jesus. It is absolutely wonderful to know that you have eternal life. Not wish, hope, think, but **know** without a doubt, that you are ready to go home and be with Jesus forever.

BUT I HAVE ALREADY BEEN BAPTIZED!

You may be wondering why I have titled this chapter, "but I have already been baptized." Before we get very far into this lesson, you may start saying this very thing. Perhaps you have already said this to someone else.

The devil seems to work real hard on keeping people confused about baptism. Baptism is an issue that many Christians never completely understand or settle in their hearts. So let's clear up all confusion.

First of all, the word baptism means to "immerse, plunge, to dip in or under or to sink." All through the New Testament, baptism followed a person's born again experience. It never preceded it.

Read Acts 2:41. What did the new believers do after they were saved?

Read Acts 8:12-13. What did these new believers do?

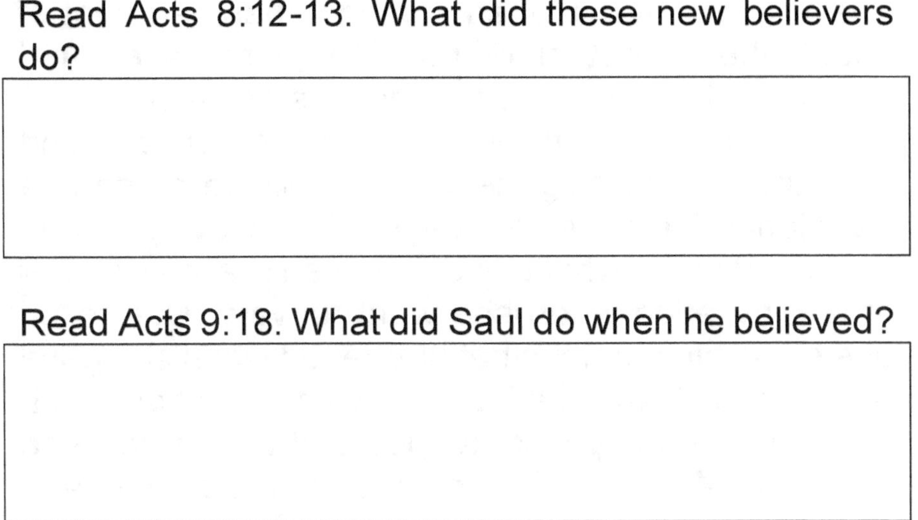

Read Acts 9:18. What did Saul do when he believed?

There are several more references in the New Testament where we see baptism following a true profession of faith. The scriptures plainly teach that after a decision to know and follow Jesus, you must be baptized, immersed, etc.

So where does the confusion come in? It usually comes in with someone who was already baptized but was not truly born again. They may have walked an isle or made a profession of faith, but were never really saved. The devil tells them that their baptism was sufficient.

If you made a decision but your life did not change or Jesus did not take charge of your life and you were baptized, that baptism was not valid. A true baptism according to scripture comes after and only after someone was converted.

I have even seen it when someone has had a lot of doubt about whether or not they were saved and made another profession of faith just to clear up any doubt and followed through with being baptized and all of the doubt was gone. My wife, Michelle, made a decision to follow Jesus at age 10. However, no one explained to her what she did or even prayed with her at the invitation when she went forward. Due to no one explaining to her what happened when she gave her heart to Jesus she had always had a lot of doubt. She was even baptized at age 10. It wasn't until she was in her 40's that she got tired of all the doubt and decided to be baptized again. This time she understood what baptism was all about. I was pastoring a church at the time and baptized Michelle. Her testimony was, after being baptized, that she never doubted again. To have peace about your decision to follow Jesus is worth being baptized again. Don't let pride stand in the way. Don't worry about what other people might say. Do what pleases the Lord.

Part of the command Jesus gave his disciples just before he ascended into heaven was to baptize all believers. Baptism is a command from Jesus, to enable believers to publicly announce the fact they have given their hearts to Jesus and are not ashamed of Him.

Baptism symbolizes:
- *Spiritual cleansing.*
- *The burial of the past. It is like attending your own funeral to celebrate the death of the old lifestyle.*
- *A resurrection to the new life.*

Based on the Bible, baptism is NOT for infants or anyone who does not understand what they are doing. Baptism is for believers who are old enough to understand they have repented of their sinfulness and desire to walk in NEWNESS OF LIFE.

Read Romans 6:3-4. In your own words write what this verse says about baptism.

The Bible teaches that baptism MUST follow your salvation experience. It does not matter how many times you have been immersed or baptized in water, if you were not BORN AGAIN, all you did was get wet; you were not scripturally baptized. Baptism is a picture that your old man died and you now walk in a NEWNESS OF LIFE. Many people have the their baptism experience out of order. Get this straight and watch what God does in your life!

Since baptism is symbolic of you dying to your old life, being buried (attending your own funeral), and then being raised to walk in a brand new lifestyle, it is obvious that baptism must follow a radical change in your life. If you were baptized before you were walking in this newness of life, you must be baptized again to be lined up with what the Bible teaches.

If you recently got saved, talk with your pastor and make sure you set up a time to follow what the Bible teaches you to do. Before we move on to the next lesson, I want you to think about when you knew, that you knew if you died you would have gone to heaven. When do you know for sure you settled your eternal issue? Be totally honest with God and yourself. Here is the big question: "Have I been baptized since I came to the realization that if I died I would go to heaven?" If not, ask yourself, "Am I willing to obey the Lord and the Bible and follow Him in this step by being baptized?" If I had been baptized before, was I truly born again according to scripture?

Once you have settled your salvation in your heart and know it is in line with what the Bible teaches, then you can move on to experiencing spiritual growth. This is the fun part of knowing Jesus. It is an exciting journey to walk with Him and grow in your faith every day.

Many Christians never grow to their full potential in Jesus because they do not discipline their life to practice spiritual exercises. Spiritual growth is natural to a person who loves Jesus and knows Him as Lord. Make a decision now to follow Jesus and discipline your life to be His disciple. The word disciple means "learner," suggesting we have a teachable spirit and are willing to learn more about Him. Start everyday by telling Jesus you want to follow Him with all your heart.

TIME TO GROW:

Read 1 Corinthians 3: 1-3. This passage of scripture suggests that the believers in the city of Corinth were not spiritual, but [________________]

These believers obviously had not grown spiritually, as Paul had expected

Read 2 Peter 3:18. What does this passage command we should do?

In 2 Peter 3:18, we are told to grow in two areas. List them below.

You grow in God's grace by experiencing Him on a daily basis. You grow in knowledge by learning about Him. You do this by reading the Word of God, being tested, going to church, walking with Him and several other ways. I know you are ready to get on with these life changing basics. Remember, it is critical that you practice the principles you are about to study. So, get ready to learn how to grow in your knowledge of your wonderful Savior and Lord, Jesus Christ. There are four very basic disciplines you need to practice the rest of your life. Choosing to implement these disciplines is key experiencing Jesus in a deep and fruitful way. If you choose to apply the disciplines, you will have a journey with Jesus that will take you to heights you would have never dreamed of.

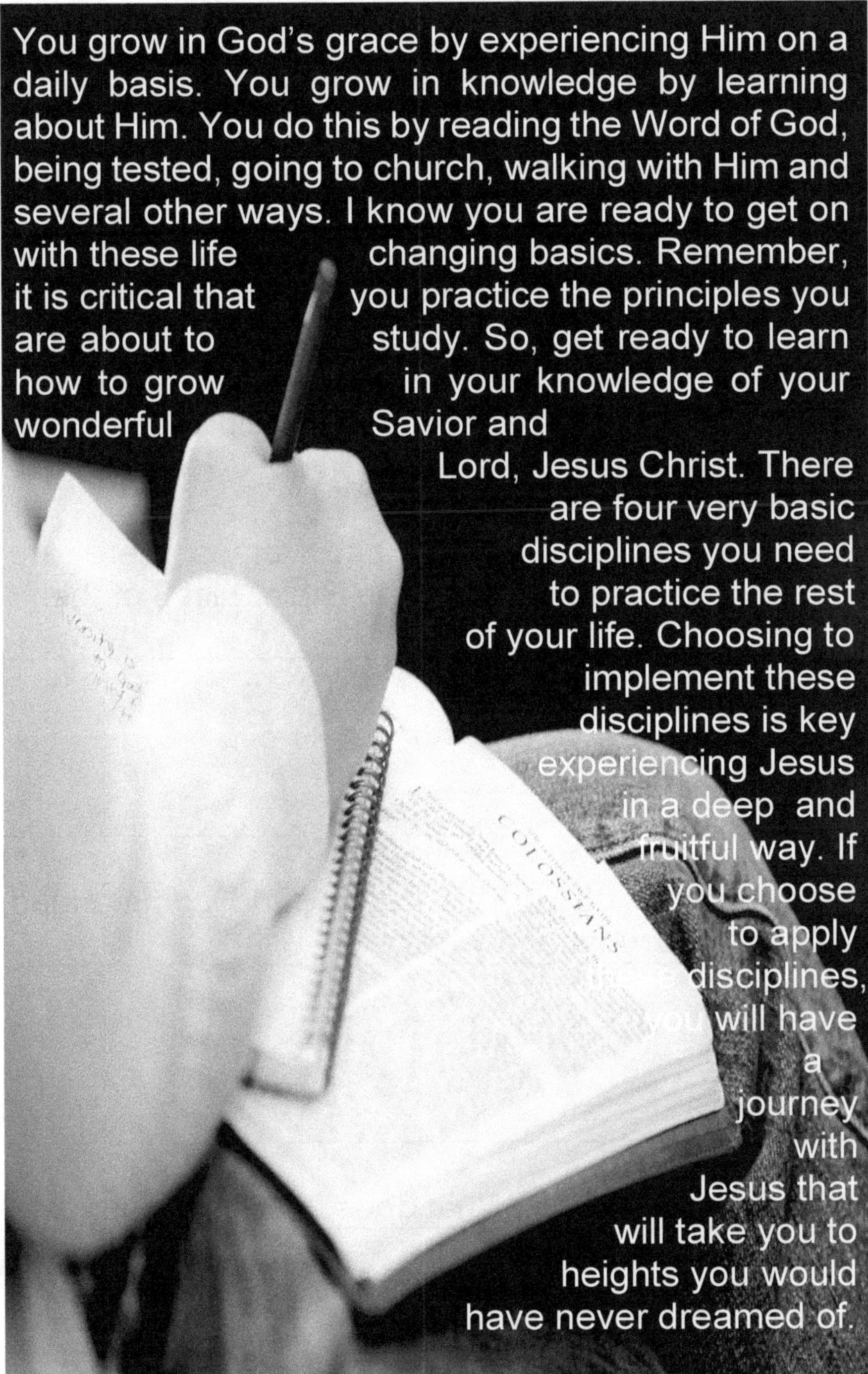

Lesson 2

DEVELOP A LIFESTYLE OF BIBLE STUDY

God wants to speak to you because you are His child. He can do this in many ways. One of the safest and most sure ways is through His word (the Bible). The Bible is full of promises for you to hold on to, blessings for you to receive, and principles for you to live by.

Read Psalm 19:7-11. In these verses there are several benefits to studying the Bible. List 3 of them below.

Read Joshua 1:8. In this verse, God commanded Joshua to do what and why?

Read 2 Timothy 2:15. What does this verse suggest?

Read 2 Timothy 3:14-15. Timothy had learned what from childhood?

According to 2 Timothy 3:14-15, what was the advantage of knowing scripture?

THE BIBLE IS FOOD

The Bible is referred to as many things to help us understand the advantages of studying it. For example, the Bible is called food.

Read Matthew 4:4. What is the Scriptures referred to in this passage?

The spiritual man must have much more than just physical food to grow.
He must have a good diet of the Word of God. The spiritual man inside of you needs spiritual nourishment. Just like your physical body needs food to fight off diseases, your spiritual life needs nourishment to resist temptation and other attacks of the enemy. It is absolutely critical of you to study the Word of God on a regular basis.

Read 1 Peter 5:8. What does the devil desire to do to you according to this verse?

The Bible tells us NOT to be ignorant of the devil's tricks (2 Corinthians 2: 11). In Ephesians 6:11, we are warned about the wiles or schemes of he devil. One of the best ways to learn how the devil seeks to destroy us is to read the Word of God.

You MUST know the Word of God to battle against the devil. In Ephesians 6:17, the Bible is called the Sword of the Spirit. This passage teaches us the Bible is a weapon to be used against an enemy. The better you know the Word of God, the more of a threat you become to him. He is out to trick you and cause you to turn away from Jesus, but your knowledge of the Word will keep your paths straight.

So far, we have learned the Bible is called food and a sword. It is for nourishment and a weapon to be used to stand against the devil. You will learn many other names for the Word as you study. Hopefully you see how important a regular Bible study time is toward providing you with the key to rising to your full potential in the Lord. I encourage you to set aside a regular time to study the Word of God. Be faithful and consistent and you will enjoy the benefits. If you do not schedule this as a part of your daily routine, you will never develop this discipline. Then you lose out on more than I have time to list in this manual.

You may choose to have a specific study time everyday or at least 5 days a week. I suggest starting with 5 days a week for about 20 minutes a day. Remember, it is not how much you read, it is how much you take in. Focus on hearing what God is saying to you during this time.

Write a few sentences about the importance of regular Bible study.

Write 2 Timothy 2:15 in the space below.

Let me give you a few tips when you study the Bible. In studying the Bible, ask the following questions:
Is there a promise I can claim?
Is there an example I need to follow?
Is there a command I need to obey?
Is there a sin I need to confess and forsake, or a sin I need to be guarded from?

Some helps in studying the Bible might be a Bible dictionary, a concordance, modern translations of the Bible, and commentaries. You should consider starting a personal library of Bible study helps. This is the difference between reading and studying the Bible. Now let's move on to lesson 3.

Lesson 3

THE IMPORTANCE OF PRAYING REGULARLY

Read Matthew 6:6. Notice Jesus says, when you pray, not if you pray. Jesus is assuming that you DO pray. He tells you to get away from the hustle and bustle of society where you can have some privacy with Him.

Read Matthew 6:7. Jesus tell us what in this verse?

Read Matthew 14:23. Even Jesus had to get away to pray. How much more should you and I? Read Matthew 19:13. What did Jesus do in this verse?

Read Luke 6:12. Here we see Jesus praying all night. He prayed all night before He was to choose His disciples. How much more should you and I pray before we make decisions?

Read Luke 22:40. Jesus told his disciple to do what so they would not do what?

Read Romans 12:12. This passage tells us to be [____________] in prayer.

Read Philippians 4:6. Here we are told to [____________] by prayer.

Read Colossians 4:2. What should we be DEVOTED to?

Although the Bible makes it very clear that we are to be a person of prayer, this is one of the hardest and most neglected disciplines in spiritual growth. An old hymn give us some good insight:

Oh, what peace we often forfeit,
Oh, what needless pain we bear.
All because we do not carry
Everything to God in prayer.

Prayer should be a vital part of your life. Many times, Christians get very discouraged and do not feel God is hearing them. They often feel God is not answering their prayers. Let me assure you that God hears every one of your prayers. Be thankful He does NOT answer every one of your prayers the way you think He should. Just be faithful to the things God has called you to, remembering that prayer is one of those things.

Prayer is simply "talking to God." God loves you deeply and wants you to spend time talking things over with Him. He desires this more than you will ever know. He longs to be with you in prayer time. He is already impressed because you know Him and love Him. He already knows all about you, and is crazy in love with you. He simply wants you to be dependent on Him for everything. Just like your Bible study time, you will have to schedule a regular prayer time or it will not happen. Combine your study time with your prayer time. Set aside a certain amount of time that you dedicate to God for spending time with Him in prayer and Bible study. I promise you will be charged up in your spiritual life. I wish I could let you know how much this will change your destiny. This time you spend with God is the most important time of your day. You should do these two things together. Get ready for a huge blessing. It is awesome.

PRAYER PLAYBOOK:

When it comes to praying, here is a tool that has helped me immensely.

1. First list the areas you feel you should pray about on a regular basis. - Your list may have things on it like; family and friends I want to see saved, myself, church leaders, special needs, my Christian friends.

2. Now let's organize this prayer time into a chart for you to keep in your Bible for regular reference. You can use this each time you have your special prayer time.

If you will pray about three minutes for each of these areas, you will have around an eighteen minute prayer time. This is a lot of time for most new believers. Don't be as concerned about the time as much as covering each area. Sometimes you will pray more for an area or two, sometimes less. This is just a guideline to keep your mind from wandering. Just make your time with Jesus real and honest.

Note: You may want to tear this out and put it in your Bible and use it as a marker for the area that you are reading in.

So far we have covered two major areas of Christian discipline. Bible study and prayer time. Make a commitment to be faithful in these areas and you will see major spiritual growth. Let me give you some great advice. The devil hates it when you spend time alone with God. The devil will try very hard to distract you from this area.

There will be times when your time alone with God seems very dry and useless. Do not let the devil sell you on this lie. Be faithful, even when you may not have any feeling. It is not about feeling, it is about spending time with God. There will be times your quiet time will be full of excitement. No matter what you feel, every time you spend time alone with God it is changing you and things around you.

Here is a warning of something that may happen. Many times when we discover something helpful to our Christian walk, we have a tendency to make it a rule. God NEVER wants us to spend time with Him because we have to. He wants us to do these things because we love to and want Him. Remember, this is all about our relationship with God. We are doing these things to get to know Him better. Practice these things from a sense of delight, and not duty.

I spend time with my boys and my wife because I love them, not because I have too.

It would grieve them if they thought I was only spending time with them because I had to.

Write a sentence or two about the importance of you having a regular time in prayer with God.

You are doing so good. I know by now you are experiencing God in a very special way.
Now to our next lesson.

Lesson 4

The church is not a human institution. It was established by Jesus Christ Himself (Matthew 16: 18). It is Christ's body on earth through which He extends His influence. Read Colossians 1:18. It is through the church that you will receive care, protection, fellowship, encouragement and spiritual development. Read Acts 2:42-44. The church is where you will come to understand the implications of your Christian life. Read Ephesians 4:11-15. The church is the place to start serving and using your gifts.

Read Colossians 1:18. What is Jesus' relationship to the church?

Read Matthew 28:19. What is Jesus' major purpose for His church?

Read Ephesians 4:11. What men have been given to the church and for what reason?

Read 1 Thessalonians 5:12-13. According to this verse what should your attitude toward your pastor be like?

Read Hebrews 10:25. What are we not to do according to this verse?

If you will operate on commitment and not on feelings or convenience, half the battle will be over. If you ever want to know what is the right thing to do, simply ask yourself this question. Your church family should become your new family and where you develop community. Be faithful in spite of anything you think should be different and God will honor your faithfulness. What would Jesus do?

Lesson 5

Read Matthew 4:18-19. In this passage of scripture, Jesus was calling His disciples to follow Him. He also told them what the outcome of following Him would be.

In the space below, write one of the results of following Him.

When Jesus said, "follow me and I will make you a fisher of men," what do you think he meant.

One of the best ways to become a fisher of men is to hang out with Jesus. Spending time with Him always results in you caring for what He cares for: lost people becoming saved.

Jesus is still concerned about people eternal destiny. As the disciples followed Jesus, they saw Him as he reached out to others on a consistent basis. They saw Him reach out to Nicodemus, a Samaritan woman at the well, a demonized person who lived in a cemetery, a woman who had a severe bleeding, a woman caught in adultery, a tax collector and the list goes on and on. Just read the New Testament and you will find His heart is reaching the lost.

The Bible says,
"Jesus came to seek and save the lost
(Luke 19:10)."

IMPORTANT NOTE:
There is a lot of deceptive discipleship today. Always know that any discipleship should always include tools that enable us to reach the lost more effectively.

The Bible teaches we should be fishers of men! This is an important part of your spiritual growth.

The last thing Jesus told His disciples before He ascended to heaven was, "Go ye therefore to ..."This is referred to as the Great Commission. This is one of Jesus great commands. I believe He meant it. Don't you?

If you read the book of Acts, you will find people being saved on almost every page. That is our example of what the church should be like.

The best and most powerful way to witness is to share your testimony of how you got saved. Practice giving sharing your story in about 5 minutes. Follow this outline to help cover the main part.

First, tell what you were like before you met the Lord. Then, tell what led you up to the point of giving your life to Jesus. Finally, tell them the difference Jesus has made in your life. Write your testimony in the space below:

Another way to witness, that is very effective, is to hand out Gospel Tracts. If you do not know what a Gospel Tract is, ask your pastor or go to a Christian book store and purchase some. Handing out tracts is like sowing gospel seeds. If you sow enough seeds you will get a harvest. Today a lot of people who do not witness are against them. However, the church I pastored handed out 850,000 in just 14 years and we got them back from 23 different states and 4 different countries saying they prayed to be saved. Don't listen to the naysayer.

A sure way to limit your spiritual growth is to keep the Good News to yourself and not witness. But a great way to experience incredible growth is to open your mouth for Jesus. If you encounter a place where it is not suitable to open your mouth, you can leave them a tract that tells them how to meet Jesus. When you really meet Jesus, you will want everyone you meet to know Him also.

Read Matthew 5:13.

Jesus said you are the [   ] of the [   ]

What good is salt if it loses it's tastiness?

One good purpose of salt is it makes people thirsty. We are to be continually making people thirsty for Jesus. How can we do this? The best way is the way we live. If people see Jesus in us, they will want what we've got. If we are going to be the salt of the earth, we are going to have to be shaken out of our salt shakers (churches).

Read Matthew 5:14-16. In the space below, write what you think these verses are saying.

[   ]

If we are going to change our world, we need to make people thirsty for Jesus, and shine brightly for Jesus. This is very easy for a Christian. All you have to do is let Jesus live in and through you. Salt does not have to try to be salty, it is naturally; all it has to do is be salt.

Light does not have to try to shine. It is naturally; all it has to do is be light. It is the same thing with being a witness. It is the most natural thing for a Christian to do.

The way we can see people come to Jesus is to just be what God has destined us to be. He said, "YOU are light, YOU are salt." You don't have to try to be this; Jesus said you are this. All day today, be who Jesus said you are.

In order to be a witness for Jesus, let me share some things that have helped me.
Be real.
Be honest.
Be sensitive to people.
Be faithful to Jesus with how you live.

Before you complete the Connect With Jesus manual, there is a very important assignment. Witness or evangelism is all about being nice and loving people. When we are nice and love people, a door will open to share the Good News.

ASSIGNMENT

Get 5 Gospel tracts and hand them to 5 different people. Make sure you smile. Find someone you can share your 5 minute testimony with. End your story with these 2 questions.
a) Has anything like this ever happened to you?
b) If you were to die today, do you know for sure you would go home and be with Jesus?

CONGRATULATIONS

You have now completed your Connect With Jesus course. Remember, all you have studied here will do you no good if all you did was learn it. You must apply each and every ingredient. The quality of your Christian life will be largely determined by whether or not you decide to apply these Life-changing principles. The rest is up to you. I want to congratulate you for completing the course, for having the discipline to stick with this study to the end. You have proven yourself to be concerned about being all you can be in JESUS. You are off to a great start. Live for JESUS everyday and never, never, never, EVER give up. Jesus loves you more than you could ever possibly know.

Evaluation

Please take a few minutes to let us know how you have benefited from this Connect With Jesus manual. We sincerely appreciate your time and opinion.

We are very interested in how this information has affected your knowledge in the Word, the part it has played in helping your establish a quiet time, and any other areas in your life where this training may have helped you grow in your Christian walk. We are also interested to know how you think this information can help others. Please give us your suggestions for future material we could provide to help you grow.

Please send your evaluation of this study manual to:
Don Babin Evangelistic Assoc Inc.
4747 research forest dr #180-287
The Woodlands, Texas 77381
903-277-8841

Next Step

Being baptized is a chance for you to take a monumental stand for Jesus. Not only are you obeying what Jesus said to do concerning baptism, but you are also saying to your church friends, that you have surrendered your life to Him.

The Sunday that you are baptized is also a great opportunity for you to see many of your family and friends come to church. On the next page you will find spaces for you to fill in your family and friends name, address, e-mail address and phone number. We encourage you to list as many of them as you possibly can.

List your neighbors, close family members, relatives, work partners, and friends. We will send them a first class invitation inviting them to your special Sunday service when you are baptized.

We will let them know how honored you will be to have them come and be seated with you on that special day.

At the service we will have a short worship time, baptism and a brief message on how to be saved and come to know Jesus as your Lord and Savior. This could be a service you will never forget. Think of all the people you love that could meet Jesus that day.

Practical notes:
Please take the time to fill out the form. Prayerfully do this. Then you will be asked to come to a short class on baptism, where you can turn in those names. The church will mail the invitation for you. The week before the Sunday you are baptized we would like for you to call your list and remind them how important it is that they come and sit with you.

God is beginning to do great things and has so much more He wants to do for you.

Invitation List

Fill this out as soon as you can and turn it into the church office, or bring it to the baptism class.

FIRST NAME		LAST NAME	
ADDRESS			
ZIP		CITY	
E-MAIL			
PHONE #1		PHONE #2	

FIRST NAME		LAST NAME	
ADDRESS			
ZIP		CITY	
E-MAIL			
PHONE #1		PHONE #2	

FIRST NAME		LAST NAME	
ADDRESS			
ZIP		CITY	
E-MAIL			
PHONE #1		PHONE #2	

FIRST NAME		LAST NAME	
ADDRESS			
ZIP		CITY	
E-MAIL			
PHONE #1		PHONE #2	

FIRST NAME		LAST NAME	
ADDRESS			
ZIP		CITY	
E-MAIL			
PHONE #1		PHONE #2	

FIRST NAME		LAST NAME	
ADDRESS			
ZIP		CITY	
E-MAIL			
PHONE #1		PHONE #2	

FIRST NAME		LAST NAME	
ADDRESS			
ZIP		CITY	
E-MAIL			
PHONE #1		PHONE #2	

FIRST NAME		LAST NAME	
ADDRESS			
ZIP		CITY	
E-MAIL			
PHONE #1		PHONE #2	

FIRST NAME		LAST NAME	
ADDRESS			
ZIP		CITY	
E-MAIL			
PHONE #1		PHONE #2	

FIRST NAME		LAST NAME	
ADDRESS			
ZIP		CITY	
E-MAIL			
PHONE #1		PHONE #2	

FIRST NAME		LAST NAME	
ADDRESS			
ZIP		CITY	
E-MAIL			
PHONE #1		PHONE #2	

9 781542 486415